Organizing Your Home With

SORT and

SUCCEED

*Five Simple Steps to Stop Clutter Before It
Starts, Save Money & Simplify Your Life*

....

Darla DeMorrow

Blue
Tudor
Books

Published by
Blue Tudor Books

Blue
Tudor
Books

BlueTudorBooks.com

ISBN 978-0-98337-2-325 (print)
ISBN 978-0-9833723-3-2 (ebook)
Library of Congress control number: 2018900100

Printed in the United States of America

Information in this book is presented for informational purposes, and is not intended to
constitute professional, legal, financial or other advice. The material may include information,
products or services by third parties. The author and publisher do not assume responsibility
or liability for any third party material or opinions. Information is provided without warranty,
and readers are advised to do their own due diligence.

CONTENTS

....

CHAPTER 1

Cure Your Clutter Troubles

....

This book is not like any other organizing book you've ever read. That's a big claim, but here are some big differences so you know what to expect.

This is a step-by-step system that doesn't just apply to physical clutter, although the physical clutter in your life is probably why you picked up this book. The SORT and Succeed system applies to everything in your life including papers, digital information, time management and even money.

This isn't just a collection of tips. I'm going to guide you through a step-by-step system with laser focus, detailed steps and hopefully more than a few chuckles.

You'll feel like you have a professional organizer there with you. You should be able to go tackle an organizing project on your own with this system about an hour from now. But if you decide you would rather work together with an empathetic, skilled guide so you can get results even faster, check out the National Association of Productivity and Organizing Professionals (https:// NAPO.net) for your local professional organizer in the USA. Professional organizers like me are located in every state and across the world. There are similar professional associations in Australia, Brazil, Canada, Japan, the UK as well.

It's realistic. You might have read other guides and thought, "Well that works for the author, but it won't work for me, my house or the part of the country where I live." I've worked with homeless families, millionaires, celebrities and lots of folks in between. Guess what? Organizing challenges—and their solutions—are surprisingly similar at all socio-economic levels, no matter what the size of the house, condo or apartment. You CAN make changes. My hope is that you will.

This book also contains some scientific study results to explain what you already know intuitively about organizing. Struggles with organizing are real, and they are brain-based. You can stop feeling like disorganization is a personal moral failing. It's not just you that struggles with organization. Sometimes it's an uphill battle against nature. With the help of scientific findings, you can understand a little of why it's easy for you to organize other people's stuff and why it's hard to organize your own.

This book, and the organizing system you'll start using right away, helps you make room for angels. If a person or opportunity shows up unannounced at your doorstep, you'll be confident that you can invite them in without fear or embarrassment. Sometimes angels are people we know, and sometimes they are strangers or new friends. Wouldn't it be a shame to turn away an angel accidentally just because of your clutter? Organizing is only worth doing if something amazing is going to come of it, and amazing comes from relationships, not things.

With the help of this book and the SORT and Succeed system, you can get the *stuff* out of the way so you can be with the people you want to be with, without irritation, guilt or tears.

Also, it's short. You wanted results, right? You'll be ready to SORT and Succeed in about an hour from now. This book is designed to be read in about one hour, start to finish, but you don't have to read it all in one sitting.

It will be easy to refer back to when you are in the middle of your organizing projects.

And there are some free downloads noted throughout the book that you can use as cheat sheets for each and every organizing project. So settle in with your favorite beverage, set the timer for an hour, and start planning what your new life will be like when you are more organized.

Get organized and stay organized by learning this system, learning to stop unnecessary stuff from coming into your life and learning to let go of perfectionism and minimalism ideas that aren't for you.

WHAT ORGANIZING CAN HELP YOU ACCOMPLISH

Who is cheering you on? I am! I'm writing this book with YOU in mind. In the last decade-plus, my team and I have worked with so many amazing people who have been able to succeed with their own life goals because of the success they have had with organizing. In the best cases, we work ourselves out of a job. Even when that doesn't quite happen, people report being much less stressed, more in control, much more productive and usually better off financially. These next stories are about just a handful of real people who were able to SORT and Succeed.

-After a nearly 30-year career as an executive assistant, R. had recently retired and was really battling the clutter in her home. She had always promised herself that she would get organized after retirement, but two years later, she was more overwhelmed than ever. She wasn't doing what was really import-ant to her, which was connecting with her friends, family and people in her church. She was flustered with the thought of her adult sons returning for a visit because the guest room was nowhere ready for a guest. She could barely see the dining room table. She had put off starting to get organized for years, but she made amazing progress in just hours when we started working together because we worked through a logical five-step system. She used our system to work her way through all of the rooms on her first floor, and she used the same approach to go through the same process again and again in other spaces in her home. Success in her case meant finding and finally giving away the gifts and greeting cards that had built up as clutter in her home, but were meant to bring happiness to her friends.

-J. is a small business owner who called us after years of struggling with disorganization. He is a very accomplished and compassionate person, but he also has ADHD. He was drowning in business receipts and unfiled tax returns going back several years. Getting started was a big roadblock. There were always so many interesting and exciting things that he wanted to do instead. He allowed us to organize his receipts by years, which meant that he could finally meet with his accountant and file taxes. Not only was he able to reduce and release mounds of paperwork, but he was able to finally reset his business to use an electronic accounting system. That meant that he could stop worrying about losing paper receipts and paying bills late. His wife was thrilled to get the guest room bed back for guests, of all things. He will tell you that he'll always be scattered, so he continues to meet with me monthly, but instead of being completely overwhelmed, it only takes about an hour each month to systemati-cally deal with his business bills, mail, filing, computer backups and accounting check-in.

-M. is a young professional who found herself stuck at work and stuck at home. Neither her office nor her home felt good to her. She admitted to wasting a lot of time online as a distraction from the overwhelming project of getting organized. Her office was covered in loose piles and cardboard boxes stuffed with paper. She balked at the idea of ordering more filing cabinets because she didn't want to feel closed in by them. She was dragging at work every day and didn't feel motivated to make changes. She had a major breakthrough when she realized she didn't have to be motivated to make changes. She committed to starting the work despite having low energy, and seeing the changes motivated her to reach her goals. She got her stacks off the floor and organized everything into new filing cabinets. She chose a warm color scheme and decorated around the filing cabinets, so they felt purposeful and stylish. By reducing the visual clutter, her office became a lot more cozy. Even her manager and co-workers took notice. They started coming to her for productivity advice! As she continued to tweak her space over the next few months, she found she was able to better concentrate throughout the day, which meant she was less drawn to wasting time online. While this work would have been easy enough for my team and me to do in a few sessions, we couldn't work hands-on in this situation because it was a high-security office environment. Instead, M. learned the SORT and Succeed steps in my office and did the physical work herself, at her own pace. Having seen the process in the office, she repeated the same steps in her home, and she created a wonderful, welcoming space there, too. The last time we talked, she said she's confident that she can repeat this process again, having learned the steps that will allow her to stay organized.

Everyone can achieve success with the right steps. Through this short book, you'll learn the five simple steps to help you organize nearly everything. You'll learn how to:

Start with a written plan

Organize into groups

Reduce, release and reset

Tweak and enhance, and then

SUCCEED and celebrate.

You might have noticed that motivation isn't part of the equation. There is no M in SORT and Succeed. Even if you feel like the forces of the universe or your own inner demons are working against you, if you follow these steps, you WILL make progress. You don't even have to be good at organizing. In fact, it's completely okay if you believe you are not good at organizing. Rely on these steps to guide you. Just like these people above, you have everything you need to get organized right now. Keep reading.

WHO SORT AND SUCCEED IS FOR

I didn't want to write just another organizing book. It's very common for my team and me to find five, ten or more organizing books when we do hands-on organizing work. As one client put it, she had become an expert on just about every organizing system, but she still had a cluttered house. She needed a better way to organize her life without feeling guilted into impractical minimalism, unattainable Pinterest-fantasy or pricey organizing gadgets.

There are some excellent books by colleagues, many of whom I personally know and highly respect, on my website's shopping page http://heartworkorg.com/shopping/. But before you bought one more book, this book, I wanted to make sure that it was truly what you needed.

In 2005, HeartWork Organizing evolved from my helping my neighbors with what I loved to do … turn a house into a home. I had just left a long corporate career in a big soul-less cubicle farm, and I was obsessed with home improvement. Corporate work moved at the pace of the glaciers. With organizing, I could make huge changes in just a few hours! It was intoxicating. I couldn't stop working because it never felt like work. My friends and neighbors asked for help with painting rooms, fixing doorknobs and clearing the clutter. I absolutely loved helping them reduce their frustration and create a wow space. In the last decade, HeartWork Organizing has grown to a team of people, applying logical thinking to creative projects to make any house into a home you can love right now.

We've loved working side by side with clients to bring them closer to a more peaceful life through organization, but I knew that we could do even more to help more people. That's why I turned the system that we use every day into this book...for YOU.

When you bought this book, you didn't just get something to read. You gained a tribe. A cheerleader. And your own personal problem solver. That's because I am not only going to help you complete your organizing project, but I want to see the results. That's right! I want you to go from this very page, to solving your problems, to a standing ovation from me and others who are on an organizing journey. I really and truly want you, dear reader, to be in touch through our private and free Facebook group. https://www.facebook.com/groups/heartworkorganizing/ Facebook has been a great way to connect with a community who encourages each other and to connect with me directly for specific advice. I'm here for you, wherever you find yourself on your organizing journey.

I created SORT and Succeed for some of the most amazing people I've been blessed to work with over the years.

- The Wishful DIY-er will use the tools and steps of this system to finally git'erdone.

- The Successful Overachiever will learn how to fit an organizing project into the day.

- The Chronic Procrastinator will finally get started.

- The Scattered Chaotic will finally learn how to stay on track through one organizing project after another.

- The Busy Entrepreneur will learn how to be more profitable through better organization.

- The Hopelessly Overwhelmed will learn how and when to get help in person, so you don't have to go it alone.

- The Cluttered Executive will appreciate the five-step plan that lays out what to expect a professional organizer to do for them when they hire one.

Are you one of these people? Are you all of them? Well then, let's get started.

WHO SORT AND SUCCEED IS NOT FOR

Everyone can benefit from organizing, but I've got to be honest, this book may not be for you. There are a few very specific conditions where another resource might be a better fit. More than anything, I want you to get the results you need, even if that means you need to seek a solution outside this book. Before you spend one more minute with me, check to see if this is you:

- If you are looking for cleaning tips, we're getting organized first. Cleaning comes after getting organized with SORT and Succeed.

- If you've been diagnosed with a hoarding disorder, please seek clinical help before hiring a professional organizer.

- If you've been diagnosed with depression or a personality disorder, please enlist your therapist to help reach your organizing goals. You can both use this system as a roadmap. Contact a local professional organizer to work in a team approach with your therapist for best results.

- If you are looking for generic organizing tips and tricks, this isn't it.

- If you are looking for an easy solution to organize your entire life in 30 minutes with no thought or effort, good luck with that.

LOSSES HURT
about twice as much as gains make you feel good

Take the guest room, which we are often called to organize. A cluttered guest room is usually covered in personal memorabilia, half-finished craft projects, supplies for unfinished home repairs, old clothes and potentially important papers. Does that describe a space in your home?

Even though the brain's rational area, the prefrontal cortex, causes you to buy this book or call a professional organizer with the best intentions of turning the storage room back into a proper guest room, the possibility of hosting guests someday is almost always a weaker emotional force than the sense of loss around the things that are already in the room, even if they are only somewhat valuable. Your emotional brain is always looking at the stuff in your home and screaming out, "No! I can't live without that! What if I need it someday????"

This might explain why we so often park $30,000 cars on the driveway, while we store $3,000 worth of junk in the garage.

Once you know there are different parts of your brain including the amygdala and prefrontal cortex yelling at different volumes, so to speak, you have a very powerful tool at your disposal. Tom Valeo's article called *When Labeling an Emotion Quiets It* suggests that the scientific research backs up this idea that you are not held hostage by your emotions. Simply labeling them can change or quiet them.[3] Once you know that the endowment effect causes your brain to value things that exist in your home *right now* much more than the exact same things you don't own, you can overcome the impulse to keep things you may not even like. *You can outsmart your brain.*

You may still get stuck on an organizing project, but now you can say to yourself, "Self, I'm going to use the big part of my brain to do the right thing for my future self." Strengthening any muscle takes practice and conditioning, and you don't have to be perfect. We like to say that perfectionism is the enemy of organizing. Perfect is the enemy of good. Knowing this, you can focus on what you want in your life both today and in the future, instead of being afraid for what you might lose. Knowing how the brain works is a powerful tool in the struggle against clutter.

PERFECT
is the enemy of good

We worked with one lovely person who had more than 75 plastic and cardboard moving boxes full of books, movies and toys from his childhood. He hadn't looked at them in years, and they were sitting in his basement. The problem was that he now had a family of his own, with kids who would have loved to play in the basement. But the entire basement was off limits because eliminating those things from his life was hard, so he didn't do it. He might not have said it was painful, but other things always took priority over clearing that space. In order to clear the space, he would have to wade through and sort through each and every box. If an organizing fairy had quietly removed those items from his life and fixed up his basement, he would have been grateful and happy. But instead, he did what almost every single one of us would do, and he insisted on looking through every book, toy and game, and he made a keep-or-discard decision for each and every item, which took days. His emotional brain was screaming the whole time, "But you used to love that!!! What if you decide to play with it again??? You spent money on that!!! What if you need it someday???" Instead, he found one reason after another to reschedule and delay and avoid the whole project, therefore avoiding getting rid of (or losing) any of his clutter. Fortunately he was really committed to helping his wife start her home-based business, and we worked through the project, bit by bit, stack by stack, bin by bin.

If you've tried to organize before and didn't feel successful, it may have been in part because your brain sabotaged you. All throughout the day, the emotional brain is screaming so loudly for so long that it is just wearing down the prefrontal cortex, which the emotional brain hopes will get tired and hungry and frustrated and give up. *Who wants pie?*

When the prefrontal cortex does get tired, that's called decision fatigue, which means that the quality of decision making deteriorates after a long session of decision making or after other physical and mental exertion, according to a significant group of psychological research since the 1990's, including work by Baba Shiv and Alexander Fedorikhin[4]. Once we are mentally fatigued, we shut down and stop making rational decisions, or at least make ones that are considered poorer quality decisions. Our decisions start coming from a more primitive place in our brains, closer to the amygdala. That's why you shouldn't shop for groceries when you are hungry. Your hungry brain will grab the high calorie, heavily marketed foods, and not necessarily the best healthy choices.

Of course, that basement full of boxes, that guest room full of half-finished projects, that garage full of everything except cars, those are your things and memories and hobbies. No one, least of all me, is suggesting that you dump everything. Minimalism and empty rooms aren't the goal. Peace is the goal.

Your prefrontal cortex, the rational decision-making part of your brain, is fighting the clock, and is becoming less rational the more hungry, tired and frustrated you get. Use these strategies to be more successful.

- Tackle organizing when you are not hungry or thirsty.

- Organize when you can concentrate on the task, not when you are likely to be distracted.

- Search for and organize the most valuable treasures first, instead of making many tiny and exhausting decisions about handfuls of trash.

- Before you start a huge organizing project like the one described above, make sure you have a specific written goal that includes finding a few real treasures that you really want to find and return to your life. This will help you stay focused on what makes you happy. Think of it as a treasure hunt.

- Most of all, when you feel yourself getting emotional or irrational about the work, take a five-minute snack break, and then return to the organizing project. Your body turns the snacks into brain fuel so you can make it to the finish line.

If you think you can't change your chaotic ways, here is more science to prove you can. Through scientific experiments and observations of brain activity through MRI machines, researchers have determined for sure that the brain is changeable and capable of learning all throughout our lifetime, not just when we are children. Scientists say the brain has *neuroplasticity*, which means that the brain is able to change and adapt by reorganizing itself by forming new neural connections throughout life. Neurons are physical structures in our brain that grow, lengthen and connect to other neurons when we learn. In fact, our brains are always adapting and rewiring. It can't be stopped!

When you learn a bad habit, you are helping neurons develop and grow. When you learn a good habit, you are helping neurons develop and grow. Habits create physical structures in our brains. Have you ever tried to change a habit, but kept falling back into old habits? You might think you just aren't capable of change. You might think your brain is somehow prevented from changing.

As a matter of fact, here's proof that you CAN change. Back in 2007, the iPhone didn't exist. Do you remember? Texting wasn't an everyday thing. People only checked email from their computer. We didn't watch movies on the go or contact people using video calls. But now, just a few years later, most of us are using a very complex device many times a day and communicating with others in a way that didn't even exist just a few short years ago. By repeatedly using our phone and our favorite apps over and over, those repetitions built solid and dense brain infrastructure, and doing these things on a smartphone now seem easy.

You pick up new habits all the time, like using a smartphone. Success comes through building a habit that is meaningful to you through repetition and reinforcement. Getting organized can be a habit.

The final piece of the puzzle is using your brain's wiring to stop clutter before it starts. Don't just build a better decluttering habit. Get better at reducing the intake of stuff, activities, useless information, and even debt into your life.

You can do this.

WHAT IS AN ORGANIZING SYSTEM?

Organizing isn't about one-time cleaning or tidying. It isn't about cute, matching bins or creating a magazine-perfect picture of your living room. You are going to learn a five-step system, and you will be thrilled at how you can be successful in a very short time.

Organize yourself successfully with repeatable systems. A system is a way to do things, the same way, every time, so that you work through from start to finish. You don't waste precious energy reinventing the wheel every time. Who has the time for that?

A system supports your habits or helps you build new habits through repetition.

A system is usually comprised of a series of steps and one or more physical tools used to accomplish those steps.

A system should be followed in order, with accuracy and speed, to achieve success. This is especially true of the first project you start after reading this book.

Some people will read this and think:

- What the heck is a system?

- I'm too creative, and this sounds very stifling.

- I get too distracted to follow anything complicated.

- I have too much stuff, and I don't even know where to start!

- I've tried getting organized before, and it has never worked.

- I'm already overwhelmed, and I haven't even started.

Never fear. We'll address all of these issues, and much more, so you can stop reading and start making the changes that you crave.

WHAT IS AN ORGANIZING PROJECT?

A project is an organizing job you can accomplish in one defined block of time, by applying the SORT and Succeed system.

If you think you'll need more than about four hours to solve your organizing problem, then your project is probably too big. You'll need to break that big project into some smaller projects.

Plan organizing projects with a beginning, middle and end. By defining where to start and where to end, you build confidence that your project can be completed in less than four hours.

Why four hours? Organizing is physically and mentally demanding. Can you think of anything that you love doing for four hours straight? It's probably a short list. Now imagine working on something for hours and NOT loving it. Ugh. That's no fun. But in smaller bites with immediate results, it can be fun.

You are going to love the results from organizing, you might even end up loving your effort, but you will not start out loving the work. Start with the end in mind, and plan to be finished in about four hours or less. That means that you'll be put back together, and you'll have something to show for your work. It does NOT mean that you'll have a bigger mess than when you started. Not if you follow the system. Uh-huh, you've already been there, done that.

If you can arrange for a helper to join you, then you might be able to take on a bigger project, but that's not always true. Two people do not equal an eight-hour project completed in four hours. Three people do not mean that you'll complete a project that might otherwise take you alone twelve hours. You might become less efficient with a helper if you have to negotiate heavily with them. They might not work with the same energy you bring. You might need to stop to take care of them or teach them things, which takes time. They might not be available during the entire timeframe you need them, so starting and stopping might throw you off. Having helpers is usually a good thing, but it's not without pitfalls.

Also, we tend to eat about every four hours during the day. When you stop, leave the project area, and prepare a meal or snack, you lose momentum on your organizing project. You have to refuel. Your brain will need it. But you may never make it back to your project. Plan on completing a project, rather than leaving a half-completed mess.

CHAPTER 3

What Is The Sort And Succeed System?

....

By now you've become convinced this book can and will help you. Perhaps you've learned how your brain can work for you instead of sabotaging your organizing efforts. Now we are ready to dig into the SORT and Succeed steps in detail. As you go through this chapter, highlight or underline key ideas that can work for you.

This system to organize any area of your home or life has five major steps, and you can easily remember them with a little ditty. We've had a little song made for you, and it's posted at http://HeartWorkOrg.com/SORTSong. Download it free and play it while you organize, if it helps you get in the mood.

There is also a free printable of the SORT and Succeed system that you can download and post in your space while you are organizing. Download a handy, free printable at http://SORT.heartworkorg.com.

S tart with a written goal

O rganize by group

R educe, release, reset

Tweak and enhance

Succeed and Celebrate

START WITH A WRITTEN GOAL - STEP 1

That's right; the first step is pretty simple. In order to get an organizing project done, you must start.

Supplies recommended - You don't need any fancy supplies to get started with your written goal, just pen/pencil and paper.

- Start with a specific written goal, the smaller the better. Instead of an undefined goal like, "I'd like to organize my home office," write down something specific like, "I will clear off my desktop and file papers from the desk where I can find them again." That is probably a smaller goal, but it's also one that is do-able in just a few hours.

- Start with the end in mind. As you write down your goal, visualize your end project. Professional athletes do this. World-class performers do this. Very successful people visualize what reaching that goal looks like. What will your organized project look like when it is finished?

- Start even if you don't feel like it. You can do the work even if you don't want to. If you have ever had a monotonous office job, you know this is true. Showing up is half the battle. Show up and get started.

FIFTY PERCENT

of success comes from just showing up

- Start at the door. Don't spend time wondering where to start. Don't pick a pile from the corner. Don't start with the oldest stack. Start at the door, and move around the perimeter of the room in a circular motion. Don't overthink it. Just start at the door.

- Set a timer for 15 minutes. Most people can do anything for 15 minutes. Work distraction-free. Don't answer the phone. Don't check email. Don't have the TV on. Don't start reminiscing through pictures. You can't constantly stop to look for your misplaced coffee cup or see what's new online. Stay focused for 15 minutes, and you'll eventually be able to work up to longer sessions. If you must, search for and install an activity blocking app on your phone. You are capable of putting aside your favorite time-wasters for 15 minutes. If that just seems too overwhelming, start with five minutes. But for heaven's sake, start!

I CAN DO
ANYTHING
for fifteen minutes

- Start with a reward. Absolutely no one accidentally organizes a room. If you love to organize, then a beautiful room might be its own reward. *But you probably don't love organizing, or you wouldn't be reading this book.* Plan to reward yourself in a few hours. Pretty much any reward except a shopping spree is fair game. You don't want to clutter up your beautifully organized space, after all. Reward yourself with a special coffee. Phone a friend and brag about how great you feel. Give yourself permission to spend time crafting, get a manicure or take a stroll on a nice day. Or just give yourself permission to read a good book on the sofa. There are plenty of good rewards for an organizing project well done.

- Start with a little fun. How long has it been since you turned up the tunes full blast? Are you wearing your superhero cape? We warn our clients that we will all break out into a money dance when we find money while organizing, which usually gets a chuckle. (We routinely find hundreds of dollars hidden in the clutter!) We all laugh at the family pets "helping" when they snuggle in the bins. Whatever it takes, plan on having fun. Life is too short for the alternative.

ORGANIZE INTO GROUPS - STEP 2

This step of the process might look daunting, but don't give up here. You'll appreciate having all this information when you are deep in your organizing project. I promise!

Supplies recommended - We use things you already have, such as laundry baskets, trash baskets with clean trash bag liners, empty shoe boxes and sturdy cardboard boxes. When we run out of space, we'll use the bed, the couch, the dining room table, and even the floor to group things together until we locate some more empty bins in your stuff. We also use Post-It® notes to label quickly and temporarily.

- You can do this. In fact, you have been doing this since you were a child. Even messy kids can organize. Did you put your school supplies in your desk at school? Did you gather your baseball cards together in a binder or box? At work, do you pile your files together in or on or near your desk? Do you stack the mail at home, even if you avoid opening it?

- Set up these important bins for any decluttering project: *trash, recycle, donate and elsewhere*. We like to use medium sized boxes or laundry baskets.

- If you are working alone, you will stay more focused if you talk it out. I've seen so many people just stare at a pile, but when they pick up one item and start talking about it, they come up with a plan for it. I suggest that you say this out loud, "This is a _____ and I need to do _____ with it." Sometimes you can talk yourself through the possible, the probable and the next right thing all in about 20 seconds, if you keep talking. It might go something like this. *"These are CD's I'm just going to keep. I'll just look through them real quickly, and I see that there are artists in here that I really don't like anymore. I'd rather get rid of those. And, actually, I've already converted everything to digital, so I really only want to keep a small handful out of this box. Okay, let's donate the entire box except for these 10 CDs."* You'll go from assuming you need to keep everything to keeping only the important items in less than a minute. It goes even more quickly when things you've been storing have rotted, molded or been chewed on.

YOUR NEW MANTRA IS

This is a (_ _ _) and
I need to do (_ _ _)
with it.

- *Donate* as much as possible to one single charity. Avoid making lots of donation piles for many different organizations. Your job is to organize, not to run all over town making donations. Even worse, you don't want to end up with donation bags that never leave your home because that errand is just one more thing that overwhelms you. I've seen it happen too many times. If possible, arrange in advance for a charity to pick up on the day after you finish a big organizing project.

- The *elsewhere* bin keeps the whole project moving. It's the magic wand that you haven't had before those other times you've tried to organize. The *elsewhere* bin holds items that you want to keep, but not in the space where you found them. At the end of your project, you will move them to the rooms or spaces where they belong, but they will not get the royal treatment today. *Elsewhere* stuff can simply hang out in other rooms—unorganized—until you tackle that next organizing project. Yes, you might be moving a small pile of unorganized stuff ahead of you into another space, but more importantly you are leaving a path of organization behind you. You'll still be better off than when you started. Use the *elsewhere* bin to keep you anchored in place, and resist the urge to leave the project space. You've probably been a victim of the Bermuda Triangle of organizing before: somewhere between your project space, another room where you were trying to return a wayward item and the refrigerator, you completely forget what you were working on, and never come back to finish organizing. Use the *elsewhere* bin to gather things that need to be carried elsewhere, while you stay in your project space until the project is completed.

- Sort similar items together in their own bin or space. You might not do it perfectly or beautifully, but do it quickly. Define big categories and temporarily label them with sticky notes. Don't get lost in the small stuff. Good examples of broad categories are:
  - clean clothes versus dirty clothes
  - clothes versus shoes
  - pens and pencils versus files and papers
  - plastic dishes versus silverware
  - towels versus soap
  - toys versus puzzles

- You might also group things that belong together by location. They might look like this:
  - makeup and hair brushes to take upstairs to the master bath
  - holiday items to be carried down to the basement
  - small tools to store together in a drawer

CHAOS

Can't Have Anyone Over Syndrome

- Sort with passion. Sort with vigor. Sort with abandon. You can do this. You are a superhuman, fighting the forces of CHAOS in the universe! The fate of the human race depends on you and your ability to make piles out of mountains of chaos and disorder!

- If you can painlessly purge an item or two while you are jamming out, go for it. But if you hold on to that item for more than two or three beats, you have my blessing to keep it for the moment. Why should you just group without tossing in some cases? Simple. Making a decision on whether to keep or toss one particular black t-shirt is difficult in the absence of more information. But once we find all 20 or 30 or 50 black t-shirts you own, it's easy to identify your favorites versus the ones that are faded, stretched, torn or just fit funny. Save some brain cells, avoid decision fatigue and sort first, purge second.

- Organize the hidden stash. Once you think you are done, go get the rest of it. You probably have another stash of clothes in a guest closet.

You probably have a second desk somewhere else in the house that also has office supplies. Sure, you emptied the pantry, but what about that bag of canned goods you threw in the basement when guests came over? Go find your secret stash in that category and finish grouping it into your project.

REDUCE, RELEASE, RESET - STEP 3

By step three you probably have a big mess on your hands. You have sorted piles all over the floor, the bed, the couch and the dining room table. Most people get to this point and lose steam. They get overwhelmed. They literally do not know what to do next. Here's why YOU have a leg up. *You know you are almost done. Success is just around the corner.*

YOU

have done harder
things than this.
You will succeed at
this, too.

Supplies recommended - You don't need any fancy supplies to sort, but we do like to use 3M Post-It® notes and a dark Sharpie® pen to quickly label the piles and bins temporarily.

- Reduce. Once you have your boxes, bins and piles grouped together, then you can decide what to keep.

- Release. Believe it or not, your goal is NOT to get rid of things. Your goal is to make room for things that you love. Getting rid of things is a natural by-product of finding, showcasing and featuring things that you love. Don't waste time obsessing over things that make you cringe. Keep searching for things that make your heart sing.

DON'T JUST TOSS STUFF

Find space for things you love.

- Make decisions, one by one, about items and piles. What stays and what goes?

- As you handle your things, you might hear yourself say, "But what if I need it someday?" If you lived in a world where food, heat and shelter were your biggest problems, it would be completely reasonable to hang on to everything, just in case. But since you've picked up this book, maybe organizing is a slightly bigger problem today.

- Instead of hanging on to stuff you don't want, remind yourself what your goal is. Look back at what you wrote down in step one—start with a written goal. Writing down those goals makes them a lot less slippery. Those goals are keeping you focused on finishing the organizing project.

- Pay attention to your gut and your expressions as you go through your piles. A helper, friend or professional organizer can point out when you display strong body language or make a face. You know what face I mean. It's the face you make when you open something furry and slimy from the refrigerator. That face is trying to tell you something.

- Reset and start to admire how great it looks already. Most of your stuff probably already has a home. Reset books onto the bookshelf. Reset the office supplies in the desk drawer. Reset the clothes in the closet and the shoes in their assigned spot.

- Recycle can mean participating in your local recycling program, but we can also recycle in place by repurposing. Put on your creative thinking cap. If you keep something, why not make it work for you? It might take a day or two to come up with some clever ideas for your things like these:

  o Rather than just plopping them together on a shelf, can you incorporate books into your decorating scheme?

  o Can you use storage boxes and bins in a useful new way, like using CD bins inside a freezer to file your bags of veggies?

- o Can you put seldom-used art supplies in cardboard boxes, stack them, cover them with a throw, and turn them into an end table in the guest room?

- o Can you hang framed art, even if you have to hang it in the garage or laundry room, instead of stockpiling it under a bed?

- o Can you spray paint mismatched baskets with a single color to create uniform-looking storage?

- Redesign. Shift furniture. Create new zones for storage or activities. Freshen up the space with a new design.

- Restock when needed. If you notice that you normally have a case of printer paper under the desk, but you are out right now, be sure to save the spot, so your replacements will have a home when you re-order them.

- Rethink your problem areas and how to improve them.

- o Use hooks whenever possible to store things off the floor.

- o Take doors off of cabinets so you don't just pile stuff in front of them.

- o Use smaller containers inside drawers to make small things easier to find.

- o Put wheels on furniture and storage trunks if it would make them easier to use.

- o Add more shelves to cabinets, bookcases and closets so stacks are always short. Stacking more than two sweaters, shoe boxes or anything else makes it hard to get to the item on the bottom of each stack.

- o Add glide-out shelves to cabinets and pantries to easily reach the items in the back.

- ○ Consider *filing* your clothes in drawers instead of folding and stacking them, so you can see all items, rather than just the one on top.

- ○ Set up your home for you, even if your solutions are non-traditional. Use a dresser in the kitchen, or a loveseat in the dining room, or a storage bench as a coffee table. Adding storage where you need it means you can easily put things away if you aren't using them daily. When things are put away, they don't look like clutter.

PUT IT AWAY
if you don't use it daily

- ○ Beware of empty containers. Make sure all of your pretty baskets, bins, caddies, and even suitcases are also storing things. Don't store air.

TWEAK AND ENHANCE - STEP 4

You've dug yourself out of chaos, and the room looks like a room again. Yay! What's left for step four? Continue to make small tweaks to make sure things work really well for you. Tweak and enhance your project, and it is more likely to stay organized. Move the pencil cup from the right of the desk to the left. Swap out furniture if it's time for an update. Post a hook on the side of the file cabinet to hold your keys. Small tweaks can have a big impact.

For some people, the project isn't done until it is pretty. Step four is where you can take your project to the next level. You now know what you need to store, what the space requirements are and what the space looks like without clutter and disorganized piles. Now you can add your finishing touches.

Supplies recommended - Paint, storage and lighting can be really helpful at this stage.

- Tweak the color scheme. Color has a huge impact on how we feel about the spaces we inhabit and the products we use. Paint, swap out or purchase items that work for your color scheme.

- Tweak the style. If your style up to now has been Early Twentieth Century Basement, and you are drawn to farmhouse style, swap a few items for galvanized steel, painted glass and bead board.

- Tweak the space. This is what separates professional organizers from other people. The average person will move their belongings into one particular spot, and will call the project a failure if those items don't perfectly fit on the first try. A professional organizer, on the other hand, will move items, grouping them, shifting them, moving them from vertical to horizontal, and perhaps back again, to find just the right fit. It's like a puzzle. There usually is no one right way to store something, but we may find better ways if we keep fiddling with them.

- Tweak the storage. If everything fits but isn't easy, comfortable or safe, make some changes. Get rid of more paper. You know you want to. Add a bookshelf. Store half of a collection elsewhere and rotate it out seasonally. Go from hard-sided to soft-sided storage. Try a different type of file folder.

- Review your written goal from step one and decide what supplies you specifically need to outfit your space. You now have permission to go purchase items to complete your design, but only if you know exactly how they will be used. Don't purchase new clutter.

- Tweak the lighting. Everything may fit in the closet just fine, but if you can't see it all, you'll end up with unused or ugly or overstuffed spots. Money spent on a good electrician and improved lighting is never wasted.

- Tweak the trash. Make it easier for things to leave your life when you are done with them. Put trash cans in each room. Add a *donate* bin to each family member's closet. Add recycling bins to your home.

- Tweak your tech. Is there an app for that? Digitizing things takes up so much less space. Take pictures so you can keep the memories, without keeping the items. A client downsized what she carried in her purse by replacing her mirror, magnifying glass, shopping list and notebook with apps on her smartphone.

- You might find it next to impossible to stay organized all the time, but you can still have beautiful spaces. If you crave the types of spaces you see in magazines, hide your belongings as much as possible behind cabinet doors and use display space for beautiful things like flowers, personal photos and treasured heirlooms. Swap out how things are stored. Put your toaster in the cabinet, and display the beautiful hand painted serving platters every day, for example.

IT'S EASIER
to tweak your environment than your habits

SUCCEED AND CELEBRATE - STEP 5

Take a bow. In just a few short hours, you've completed all the steps to get through a complete organizing project! If this is the first time in a long time, or perhaps the first time ever that you've done so successfully, let me know so I can celebrate with you. I invite you to post your success to our Clutter-free Facebook group https://www.facebook.com/groups/heartworkorganizing/ each and every time you have an organizing success, whether it's big or small. Everyone needs a pat on the back now and then.

Supplies recommended - Your written goal from step one will guide you to call your project finished. Your reward can be nearly anything.

- Review your reward. What did you promise yourself as a reward when you finished your project? It's time to pay up. Enjoy.

- Rinse and repeat. Success brings more success. Yes, you are probably tired, but maybe a little invigorated, too. You might have worked long and hard enough that you'll have to sleep on it and see your work with fresh eyes tomorrow in order to really appreciate your transformation. But YOU DID IT! And you can do it again. In fact, I have no doubt that you WILL do it again.

- Pick another small project and start back at step one with a new written goal for another organizing project. Organize your things into categories. Reduce, release and reset. Go back and tweak your work until you absolutely love it. When you succeed, celebrate achieving your goals again.

AN OUNCE OF WONDERFUL

is worth a whole
mess of mediocrity

CHAPTER 4

"I Don't Know Where To Start"

COMPLETE HOME ORGANIZING PROJECTS IN THIS ORDER

By working through small, manageable projects, one by one, you can organize your whole house and have fun doing it. Every household is different, and your individual needs and hot spots should guide you. But if you don't know where to start and your goal is to organize your entire house, here is the order I recommend:

- Kitchen and Pantry

- Main storage area (basement, mudroom or garage)

- Home office

- Main living area

- Master bedroom

- Master bath

- Kids' rooms

- Kids' bathrooms

- Kids' play area

- Craft room

- Garage or secondary storage area (attic, shed)

- Dining room

ORDER MATTERS

Why start in the kitchen? Some of the top New Year's resolutions each year are to lose weight, save money and get organized. By getting organized, you can accomplish all three. If you start by organizing your refrigerator and then work your way around to all the areas of your kitchen (pantry, cabinets, shelves, additional food storage areas), you'll have a much better idea of what you own, what you like and what you don't like. Then you can make choices that support getting fit and saving money.

For instance, if you organize your pantry and find several cans of garbanzo beans (also known as chickpeas) which are nearly expired, you have a choice:

a.   You can use this food in dinner tonight with recipes like roasted chickpeas, vegetarian chili and even baked goods made with chickpeas, believe it or not.

b.   You can donate those cans before they expire and stop buying food you will not eat. Cut yourself some slack, give yourself a break from your good intentions and move on.

Either choice will get you closer to getting fit and saving money. However, if you never take the time to organize your pantry, you might not realize that you keep buying the same food, wasting time, space and money.

The kitchen is also a great first project because it can be broken down into lots of smaller projects. You don't have to organize your kitchen all at once. You can just organize one drawer. One shelf. Just inside the oven (yes, we both know stuff is in there). The entire project might take a few days or weeks, but it still can be done, little by little, with persistence and with these same five steps.

While you organize small sections of your kitchen, you can also practice NOT being a perfectionist. It just doesn't make sense to pull everything out of your kitchen all at once in order to organize it. Where would you put it? But you can pull out the contents of the silverware drawer and group spoons together, forks together, knives together. Throw away the random straws, toothpicks and sauce packets. Return the stray utensils to the utensil drawer (you can tackle that next time). Once they are out of the drawer, wipe down the inside and replace everything. That might take you 15 minutes tops, and you haven't wasted a whole day or exhausted yourself. Time to celebrate!

See? Organizing doesn't have to be all or nothing, perfect or not at all, throw everything on the front lawn like you've seen on TV. There is a better way, and it's by going through the SORT and Succeed system in projects that take you less than four hours each so you get from start to finish all in one attempt.

AIM FOR PERSISTENCE

not perfection

Once you succeed in the kitchen, head to the storage areas in your home. Many people stop organizing because they feel like they are just out of space. By organizing storage areas, like the garage, basement and mudroom next, you'll have places to store things.

After that, we'll often work on a home office. A lot of clutter builds up in home offices while it is waiting some kind of decision. Returns, things to fix, gifts, unfinished photo projects and all sorts of other stuff can usually be found in a home office. By setting up systems to handle bills and household files, we often find better ways to store seemingly random items. Getting paper and bills under control can help get other household items tamed, too.

After that, tackle the spaces that cause you the most amount of pain. The basement doesn't feel so overwhelming. Your closet can be a fun organizing project when you see results right away. Kid's areas are child's play to organize with this system. Even better, use this system to teach kids how to become organized. Start enjoying your entire home again.

WHEN AND WHY TO CHANGE THE ORDER

There are two main reasons to work with the order recommended above or to customize a prioritized list for yourself. First, just having a plan at all will help you work through your home organizing projects. Having a written list with next projects already chosen will help you stick to it, especially if you start and stop over time. You can work through your whole house in a few days, or it might take months. The important thing is to consistently make small improvements over time.

Clients often have trouble prioritizing their own projects. Can you guess what most people say is their top priority? "All of it. The whole house." That's not a prioritized plan. That's just being overwhelmed. Work from a list to reduce overwhelm.

The second reason to work from a customized, prioritized list is to identify and work on your high-value projects first. Try to pick projects that will show off immediate results and offer solid motivation for the next project. Even though you don't have to be motivated to start organizing, the more results you see, the more you'll want to organize.

The weather may dictate your project order. My company is located in the American Northeast. We generally don't organize garages from November to March, and we don't organize attics from June through September. It's just miserable to tackle those spaces at those times of the year. Your home didn't get this way overnight. Waiting a few weeks won't kill you. Plan to work on each space when it makes sense.

CHAPTER 5

Avoid Common Organizing Traps

You might think it's just you, but everyone runs into challenges when they are organizing a space. Everyone, even professional organizers like me. Don't get sidetracked by these common organizing pitfalls and traps.

GETTING DISTRACTED

It may never be the perfect time to organize, but it is always the perfect time to be organized. People love to work with a professional organizer because when they make the appointment, they block the time on their calendar, turn off the phone, and avoid distractions for a few hours. We help them be very, very disciplined for a short amount of time. You can do the same thing, even if you don't naturally have much discipline, by writing down the organizing appointment on your calendar, leaving your phone out of the room to avoid calls and texts, and setting a timer to keep you focused on your organizing task for 15 minutes or more. Avoid the TV, computer and any other noise besides low-volume music. The key is to just start. Keep starting, if you have to. If you get distracted, it's okay. I find it helpful to say something to myself like, "Okay, I was just clearing off my desk, so I need to get back to the office and finish up." Saying it out loud makes it real, almost as if someone else was giving me that kind of reminder. In other words, it's okay to talk to yourself.

IT'S BETTER TO BE READY

than to get ready

People tell me all the time that they just aren't good at organizing. Or they've gotten halfway through every organizing project they've ever tackled, but it always ended up a mess again. In all the years that I've been helping people organize, I haven't found one hopeless case yet.

If you need a cheerleader, please join our online Facebook community at https://www.facebook.com/groups/heartworkorganizing/ where you will find people who will encourage you through each and every project.

TAKING IT TOO SERIOUSLY

Laugh a little. How much fun can you have with your organizing project? Can you chuckle at the fashions that you used to wear? Every time that we find money, whether it's cash, an uncashed check, or a gift card, our whole crew gets up and does a silly money dance. If you can imagine your situation through someone else's eyes, it might be a little more than amusing. Are you still stressed about making things perfect? Do you really think you want to live in a magazine spread? It's way overrated. Your home is meant to be lived in. Lighten up.

DROWNING IN EMOTIONS

You want to laugh at those blazers with shoulder pads from the 1980's in the back of your closet, but you may feel something else instead, perhaps shame, guilt, embarrassment, sadness, pride, regret, nostalgia and more. This is completely normal, but we aren't meant to live our life in sadness, in pain or in the past. You are here on this earth for a better purpose than hoarding moth-eaten, mass-produced goods. Your emotions are yours and they are valid, but they don't have to rule your physical world, your calendar or your finances.

Too often we never even start organizing projects because we anticipate painful emotions. I've seen so many people even refuse to open a box because they are absolutely sure that what's inside is important, irreplaceable and valuable. I make them open the box anyway. (Feel free to glance over your shoulder at that pile/box/closet that you are dreading and avoiding.) When we actually open the box, it usually wasn't what we thought was in there anyway (Oh, I thought that was Grandma's china, but it's really just moldy textbooks!), or we find that it's not worth keeping (Oh, I thought that was Grandma's special glassware, but I had no idea that it got smashed to bits in the last move!—true story). Honor your past, but don't let it define your today.

GETTING OVER IT BY GETTING OVER IT

Do you wish there was more information here about dealing with emotional landmines? Here it is. This is a game changer.

How do you get over a behavior that is producing results that don't make you happy? How do you change your habits so your home isn't cluttered? How can you create a beautiful home that is a peaceful sanctuary? What if you fail? What if it's not perfect?

A smart person once told me to get over my fears by getting over them. There's no reason to stay stuck in your clutter, bad habits or any other phase of your life if you don't want to be stuck. Get over it by getting over it. Make a decision, just one decision, even if it's just the decision to open the box, to pick up the next item or to move one thing to the donation pile. Just start.

DOING TOO MUCH

Take on the right-sized project. If you've ever painted a living room or hallway, you might remember asking yourself, "Where should I stop?" In many homes, there is often no clear break from one room to the next, so it's easy to keep enlarging the project until it is overwhelming. This is called scope creep, and it can happen in organizing, too.

Have you ever started in the bathroom, only to find yourself standing in front of some closet somewhere else in your home, starting to organize that? You will absolutely be more successful by starting with the end in mind, starting with a written goal, using the *elsewhere bin* to stay rooted in place and limiting your project to somewhere between 15 minutes and four hours. When you find yourself distractedly wandering around your kitchen, you can remind yourself out loud that, "My written goal was just to organize the bathroom today before lunch." If you aren't anywhere near the bathroom, and it's thirty minutes to lunch, you still have time to rally and make it happen.

DEFERRING DECISIONS

Have you heard that clutter is delayed decisions? We bring something new into the house, or we get a letter that needs a little bit more attention than we can give it, and we say that we'll just put it down here on the counter ... for now. We intend to return in our free time and figure out where to put it or what to do with it. But that free time never materializes, and we get three more things tomorrow that will also require decisions. Catch yourself using that old lie, "I'll just put it here ... for now." Instead, deal with it now. Put things where they belong when they come in your home. Have a safe place to park unopened mail, and only deal with the mail when you have the mental bandwidth to make decisions. Teach other people in your home where things go, so you aren't the only one organizing. When you can't deal with it now, write an appointment on your calendar to come back to it, before it grows roots and becomes clutter.

MAKING THE WRONG DECISION

I demonstrate making decisions in my organizing classes. I dump a bin or drawer full of stuff on the table and ask attendees to sort the items. That's it. I don't offer any more information. One group of people might separate the pens from the pencils, and put erasers in a third pile. Another group might organize all of the pens and pencils by color. A different group might line everything up on the table, left to right, smallest to largest. Who has the right answer? They all do! When the only instruction is to sort the items, the possible solutions could be endless. Your space and the way you have always had things arranged might be ready for an overhaul. Think about sorting your things differently, so you can use your space differently. Perfection isn't the goal. There are no organizing police. Usually the only wrong decision is no decision.

DISCONNECTING FROM YOUR GOAL

Keep what you love. Because of popular home improvement shows, many people have the idea that organizing is about throwing things out. In fact, it's not. Does that surprise you?

Rather, organizing is about making space for things that you love, and being able to share things and spaces with people you love. If there's a pile, stack or plastic tub (or two or twenty) of stuff that you don't love, but you are constantly stepping over it or kicking it to the side, is it really helping you? In today's world of easy access to inexpensive consumer goods, keeping something *just in case* isn't a good enough reason if you feel overwhelmed, discouraged and flustered. The argument that you'd have to buy it again doesn't hold water. You could often obtain those items again through free online recycling groups, borrow from friends or rent if you needed them. Keep and use what you love.

Go back to your written goal, and don't get sidetracked by possibilities, the endowment effect or your emotions.

DISRESPECTING YOUR BODY'S MESSAGES

Let your body tell you what to keep. People often ask how to cut the emotional ties to their clutter. I simply mirror back to them the expressions on their faces. Do you really want to keep the wedding album from your first marriage? (That bum!) Are you really planning on needing those crutches again? (Heck, no!) Do you really want to put stuff back in the attic, after you've spent all year battling rodents? (Eew!) Would you trust your skin to these expired cosmetics from another decade? (Not on a bet!) The look on your face tells me no. Your body is sending you messages. You don't have an unlimited supply of energy to spend on stuff, so listen to what your body is telling you.

DESTROYING RELATIONSHIPS

Is your stuff controlling your house, your time, your money and your heart? Do you sometimes feel like the stuff is your master? Do you fight with family members because of the stuff? Resistance to decluttering or avoiding new clutter might really be about how you've been treated in the past or what you think is fair or valuable. You might need some extra help from a therapist or a friend who is a good listener in order to talk through what's really going on. Most stuff is just stuff, neither good nor bad. The trouble with stuff is usually how it affects our relationships with others.

CHAPTER 6

Make Lasting Changes

This is the best part of the book because this is where you change your space and change it forever.

Success doesn't mean that you'll never have to organize your space again. Success is organizing with less effort and more insight.

DAILY ORGANIZING HABITS

Somewhere along the way, we've confused *decluttering* with *getting organized*. There is no prize for the one who purges the most toys, clothes, papers and whatever is hiding in the basement. A 30-day plan to declutter your house might clear a path in the playroom, but it doesn't actually get you organized. Throwing away 75 percent of your clothes will definitely free up space, but it's just as likely to lead to a buying binge as it is to bring joy.

What makes for a life that is organized? Like everything worth doing, the answer is simple but perhaps not easy. An organized life comes from lots of small daily choices made consistently.

AN ORGANIZED LIFE

comes from lots of small choices made consistently

HeartWork
organizing

So let's not do another **30-DAY ASSAULT OF ONE-SIZE-FITS-ALL THINGS TO DO EACH DAY OR 100 THINGS TO THROW OUT NOW OR YOU WILL BE AN ORGANIZING FAILURE.** Isn't that what it feels like? Let me offer another approach ...

Organizing doesn't just happen in closets and cabinets. There are four main areas of organizing that are inter-connected:

- Space/stuff

- Time

- Information/paper

- Money

In this book, there's a definite focus on space and stuff, but there is always overlap between these categories, for example:

- If we reduce the amount of clutter in our homes (space), we spend less time cleaning.

- If we take care of important paperwork (information), we don't miss deadlines (time).

- If we use a personalized file system (information), then we don't lose the kitchen counter (space).

- Generally, if we improve in any of these areas, we find ways to save or earn money.

Clutter doesn't happen overnight, and yet popular culture has latched onto an idea that a big one-day purge will create organization, and you will be organized *henceforth and forevermore.*

In reality, clutter happens in drips and drops, and *organization happens the same way.*

Instead of a long list of big projects you should complete, one after the other with a high chance of failure, do the basic things really well. Put important things, like keys, in the same place every time. Put things away. Don't use the floor for storage. Close dresser drawers. Wipe up spills. Hang coats.

By doing these little things consistently, you create more space and time for you to be amazing at whatever you were meant to do...which is probably something besides organizing.

If you already do some of these things, great, continue doing them, and add on one more organizing action or organizing habit each day to build your organizing muscle.

With this approach, you will be more organized, and you won't have to lose a whole day of your life so you can organize your things. Or if you do schedule an organizing project, it can be for something big that allows you to get ahead, instead of just barely keeping up.

You can download a list of 31 daily habits from http://heartworkorg. com/2017/01/04/plan-to-get-organized-in-2017-and-succeed/ and check off a new item as you add it to your daily routine. By adding new habits from this list, eventually you will be doing about 31 teeny-tiny organizing actions each day. None of these items are craft projects or require you to buy anything special or take more than a few minutes. By turning lots of mini-organizing projects into daily habits, you'll be surprised at how much more in control of your life you feel. Or maybe you won't be surprised at all.

THE 80/20 RULE

The 80/20 rule, otherwise known as the Pareto Principle, was coined by the economist Vilifred Pareto in Italy in the late 19th century. He observed that only about 20 percent of the population owned about 80 percent of the land. He noted that the "vital few" seemed to have more of an impact than the "trivial many". This idea can be extended into many areas of our lives like tasks, priorities and possessions. In business we notice that 80 percent of revenues often come from the top 20 percent of customers. At home we wear 20 percent of our clothes about 80 percent of the time. When it comes to time management, we observe that about 20 percent of the things on a to-do list are really critical. The rest? Not so much. So the next time you are overwhelmed, write down all the stuff that you could be doing, then mark out 80 percent of it, focus on the critical 20 percent that's left, and you'll probably feel like you are moving mountains.

If you walk into a cluttered room, about 20 percent of your things are valuable and treasured. The other 80 percent could probably leave your life without much of an impact, not that they have to. It might be closer to 70/30, or it might be closer to 90/10, but the general principle still works. Don't let the "trivial many" overwhelm the "vital few."

Knowing about the 80/20 rule can help you break perfectionist tendancies. If the bang for your buck only comes from the 20%, then being 100% perfect 100% of the time is not only exhausting, but it's counter-productive when it keeps you from ever getting started. Be amazing at the 20% level, and you might just be happier all the way around.

SOMETIMES GOOD ENOUGH
is good enough

TWEAK AND FIDDLE

Doesn't Tweak and Fiddle sound like a great name for a band? We already talked about tweaking earlier, but it's a big part of your success. If you've ever organized a space and gave up frustrated, it's likely that your thought process went like this:

I'll gather all the kitchen towels together and put them where they've always been, in this drawer.

Oops, there are more towels than I thought.

{shove, shove}

They don't all seem to fit in this drawer.

Darn it. I'm no good at organizing!

Who wants pie???

Someone who loves organizing has a completely different internal dialogue that goes like this:

Let me just get all the kitchen towels together and see what I've got.

If they fit here, I think they should go in this drawer, because it's close to where I use them.

While I'm at it, why don't I consolidate these towels with that other stack over there?

Oops, there are more towels than I thought.

They don't all fit in this drawer.

Okay, I don't love these anymore. They can become car wash rags and get stored in the garage.

These brand new towels really aren't my style, so I'd be happy to donate these.

Now it all fits nicely in the drawer.

Let me just try them over here, in case I like that better.

Nope, better in the drawer I picked originally.

Let me see if there is a better way to fold them.

Now there's even plenty of space for towels that are in the wash right now.

Good. Looks good.

Better tell the family that towels now go in this drawer.

Not only is the process a bit different, but the organized person will tend to fiddle a bit more and check to see which possibility works best. The average person will either try to jam things into where they don't physically fit or will assume he or she just doesn't have the skill for organizing, which is just nonsense.

You can do this.

OUTSMART THE STUFF

Probably a few times in your life, you've organized something and then thought, "It's going to get disorganized in no time." Or you've thought, "I feel like I'm constantly organizing this same closet." Both of those statements are probably partially true, because the flow of consumer goods in and out of your home will continue as long as you are alive.

But we are in control of those consumer goods.

Let's talk a bit more about the brain and organizing. Did you know that the act of shopping delivers a chemical high to the brain? According to Kelly McGonigal's book, *The Willpower Instinct, How Self-Control Works, Why it Matters, and What You Can Do To Get More of It,* "When the brain recognizes an opportunity for reward, it releases a neurotransmitter called dopamine. Dopamine tells the rest of the brain what to pay attention to and what to get our greedy little hands on."[5] This chemical reaction-turned-habit is stronger in some people than others, like when it comes to shopping. But the brain doesn't just get excited about new stuff. It can just be new-to-you stuff. The brain reacts to the possibility of something thrilling on the next sale rack, in the next boutique, in the next Amazon box delivered to your door, or even the next juicy curbside trash pile that might have some good DIY materials. We get quite accustomed to these little shots of dopamine, and if we don't recognize the danger, we can train our brain to want that dopamine stimulation even more. Dopamine-seeking behavior-turned-habit can lead to acquiring more consumer goods.

Layer on another very powerful force in your brain that wants to avoid pain—or potential pain. In fact, we will do more to avoid pain than we will do to seek equivalent levels of pleasure! In the field of psychology, it's called "loss aversion," as described by Amos Tversky and Daniel Kahneman.[6] Loss aversion is your brain wanting to hold on to stuff, so you think, "I might need it someday, and if that happened it would hurt, make me feel silly or cost more if I have to replace this item." That makes perfect sense if we are getting rid of something useful, unique or expensive, like a car or gold watch. But it makes no sense when you are faced with too many free hotel shampoos or unmatched black socks with saggy elastic. Hand-dyed yarn is fun; four hundred hand-dyed skeins that prevent you from entering your craft room can simultaneously prevent you from being able to start any craft projects at all, and yet still exert a powerful emotional pull.

Pair the dopamine high with loss aversion, and then add the endowment affect you read about chapter 2, and you can see why some people feel they have real trouble with the organizing process.

If you don't perceive something as part of your endowment yet, you don't feel the need to avoid the loss of it, but you may want to acquire it anyway if you find shopping fun or thrilling. Once it becomes part of your world, look out! The brain then will work harder to avoid the pain of losing something, even if you thought you didn't really care much for that item just a short time ago. This is true for valuable items, but it also is true for inconsequential items like mass-produced five-dollar coffee cups (Thaler, *Misbehaving*).

We often use the excuse that we don't want to waste money by parting with clutter, but if you aren't using it, can't find it or you are embarrassed or physically harmed by it (as any parent who has ever stepped on a Lego® has been), then perhaps it's not really the desire to practice good financial stewardship that makes decluttering hard. The brain's physical and chemical wiring is what we're really up against.

KEEPING
CLUTTER
LONGER

doesn't make it
cheaper

Some people develop addictions to shopping, but most of us are just less aware of the volume of things that we purchase and what it does to our body chemistry and our environment.

Now, I'm not saying that you should or can stop shopping. Nor do you need to build a bonfire with your belongings.

What you can do, and what you must do if you intend to make lasting changes, is to be very, very selective about what you let into your endowment, your home, your universe of possessions. If you stop clutter before it comes home with you, there is less to declutter later.

If you've read other organizing books and wondered why you haven't been able to get organized, this might be the magic key, the silver bullet, the game changer. It is counterproductive to organize your home and still continue to bring more things into your home than you have room to store. So when you are shopping, there are some key questions to ask yourself:

- Do I already own something similar?

- Do I own something that could do the same job as what I am about to purchase?

- Can I borrow or rent this same thing instead of buying it?

- If this is a gift, do I have a specific recipient in mind, and can I deliver it to them soon?

- Do I have a specific place to store it?

- Will it cause me physical pain or expense to bring it home or move it to storage?

- Is it likely to last very long?

- Can it be recycled when I'm done using it, rather than going to a landfill?

- Can I return it if it doesn't work out?

- Can I pay for it with cash?

Annie Leonard, a noted environmental advocate, breaks down the amazingly complex consumer goods supply chain in The Story of Stuff, which illustrates how most of us get the stuff we own through global manufacturing.[7] This short video might change your life. At the very least, it might make you think about impulse purchases when you hear this frightening number. According to Leonard, "Guess what percentage of total material flow through this system is still in product or use six months after their sale in North America. Fifty percent? Twenty? NO. One percent. One! In other words, 99 percent of the stuff we harvest, mine, process, transport—99 percent of the stuff we run through this system is trashed within six months."

This does not mean that one percent of things we buy are still in use after six months, although it sure does feel like that could be true. No, it's worse than that. This quote refers to the products we buy and also the resources and materials that it took to make and deliver those products. Our trash isn't just what we put at the curb each week, but all the resources that are spent on manufacturing and distributing those items, too! Does that make you want to think twice before bringing new things in your home?

24-HOUR RULE

The 24-hour rule has saved my bacon more times than I can count. The 24-hour rule says not to make any major purchases on impulse, and take 24 hours to think it over. In 9.9 times out of ten, I've completely forgotten about that impulse a day later. The 24 hours allows me to comparison shop. Very rarely do I end up going back and making that purchase, and when I do, I'm usually very happy with it. On the other hand, I almost always regret impulse purchases.

Let's see the 24-hour rule in action. I head to the mall on a rainy day. With the kids in the stroller, I pass a fancy tea store. It's actually a perfect day for hot tea. The kids are fussy, I'm tired and I deserve a break. We pop in, take advantage of the free sample, and get hit with a seductive pitch to buy a fancy brew pot for $100 and the tea that we just sampled which, by the way, is actually a blend of two teas and a fancy sugar, all for another $50. Wow, the tea was good, but I hadn't planned on buying anything at all, and my pantry is already stocked with several months worth of tea at home. I can invoke the 24-hour rule and get myself out of there before blowing my budget.

The sales person is going to have some pretty solid-sounding information about why I need that tea or (insert consumer good of your choice). I know people who will buy something just to get the heck out of there and avoid hurting anyone's feelings. The 24-hour rule can be your bad cop, as in, "Sorry, hubby and I agreed that we have to wait 24 hours to buy anything like this so we can reach our financial goals." Every single time I've used this, it has stopped an aggressive salesperson dead in their tracks, because they wish they were that disciplined about their own financial goals.

That's all well and good at the mall, because you can come back tomorrow or next week and get the goods. But what about when it's a one-of-a-kind item, or you are traveling and won't have a chance to return to this gem? Yes, I've been there, too. For the most part, we live in a global economy, and you can still get that item 24 hours later. But when I visited New Zealand, I really, really wanted to get this beautiful New Zealand merino wool sweater. I'd never seen anything like it before. It was warm but lightweight, and it had anti-microbial properties so you practically didn't even have to wash it. Twenty-four hours later, I'd be on a plane headed home, with no chance of returning to buy the sweater. I could have justified buying it, even though the $350 sweater was waaaaaay out of my budget. I invoked the 24-hour rule, and have since researched merino wool sweaters to find some more affordable options online. And all these months later? I still might buy it ... tomorrow. My brain doesn't feel deprived or punished or restricted or any of those other things when we hear ugly words like budget. My brain is mostly satisfied that I can buy a merino wool sweater tomorrow, but in the meantime, there's less clutter in my closet.

BUY IT

tomorrow

If you are headed on vacation and really want to come home with some unique items, and you have set aside budget for purchasing and shipping them, then buy whatever your heart desires. Buy your kids special reminders of a trip. Enjoy life, for heaven's sake, if that was truly in your plan and budget. But if you have a lifetime of impulse buys cluttering your home, then the 24-hour rule can be your friend. Forty bags of clutter purging isn't going to make a dent if you (and other people you live with) are still bringing things into your house by the truckload.

ORGANIZING ELEPHANTS

Oftentimes, there is an elephant in the room, and I'm not talking about piles of clutter. There might be one or more very large items in your space, and you've tried to fight the clutter battle around them without ever addressing them. These pieces are so large that they require assistance, expense or both to remove them from your space, and you just try to get by without dealing with them.

I get it. Once something comes home with you, it can feel permanent. But if you have organized everything and still feel squeezed and cluttered, it's time to address that elephant in the room.

The family I mentioned earlier that was trying to turn their basement into space for a home-based business had a huge ping-pong table that dominated the room, even folded up. Well, the table wasn't any larger than normal. It just seemed huge in the space, like an elephant. The funny thing was that the family had not purchased the table; rather they had inherited it from the previous homeowners. They had no idea if the table even opened. Their own kids were all less than five years old, so it was going to be several years before any of them could even play. More importantly, there simply was no room to open the table, even after organizing the space. What to do with this elephant? The family was keeping it for *maybe* and *someday*, but they finally understood that they simply would not be able to keep the childhood keepsakes that mattered to them and still set up their home-based business if they did not let the ping pong table go. They called a charity service, which picked up the table, and they were able to claim the deduction on their taxes, which eventually resulted in money in their pockets.

That would have been a win on its own, but the same family had a Bowflex exercise system, too. And they had an oversized dollhouse that their youngest daughter practically could have moved into. They didn't just have one elephant in the room; they had a herd of them! They dealt with these large items, one by one.

I've seen all types of large, bulky items that literally stopped clients from organizing. Maybe you have one or two of them yourself:

- Exercise equipment
- Grandma's dining room table and chairs being saved for the grandkids
- Oversized filing cabinets, which are usually in poor shape
- A snow blower or power tools that get used once a year, if that
- A guest bed that dominates the home office and rarely gets used
- A piano no one plays
- A vintage, oversized desk with broken drawers, that catches clutter on its massive top

These elephants are space killers. In some cases, there is just no getting to the outcome you want—an organized home—without moving that elephant out. Fortunately, there has never been a better time to do this, thanks to the Internet. Here are a few ways you can proceed:

- Donate to a non-profit organization
- Sell online
- Send to auction
- Freecycle or list on another green or recycling online list
- Pass on to a family member or friend

ONE IN—ONE OUT

Simple solutions work. Instead of waiting for a buildup of stuff that needs to be organized and purged, train yourself to use the one in-one out rule every-place in your life. There was a time not too long ago when families wouldn't ever dream of having so many household goods and pantry items on hand just in case. Depression-era families would often completely wear out their clothes before they were replaced, and sometimes even then the fabric would be re-sewn into new garments for younger family members, before it would finally be used up as rags or kindling. They would practice this kind of recycling and thrift in nearly every aspect of their lives. But here in the 21st century, we've mostly lost the need for and the interest in that kind of life. Instead, we are likely to acquire something new, even when the old model still works perfectly fine. When was the last time you saw anything actually threadbare? But we might buy the newest coffee maker, kitchen appliance or home decoration, even though the old ones work just fine.

In order to manage this flow of goods into our homes, we've got to move items out of our homes at roughly the same rate as they arrive. When you buy or receive something new, move out something you already own. Sometimes you are trading up in quality, like when I bought a new blue cashmere sweater and donated a blue cotton sweater that I no longer wore. In fact, I needed the hanger that my old sweater occupied in order to store the new sweater. If you have really nice hangers and they always stay in your closet, it's easy to keep track of when you need to make a swap like that.

Sometimes a one in-one out swap isn't quite that direct. Remember when we were all switching from VCR tapes over to DVDs? Most families kept them all, and now they have closets full of VCR tapes that are good for nothing. The closet is stuffed full of VCR tapes and DVDs. And what do we watch? On demand entertainment!

One in-one out is slightly harder to manage with children, because both kids and parents can get attached to toys and keepsakes. Teach kids to orga-nize and donate right before major gift events, like Christmas and birthdays.

Children as young as five and six years old can usually be persuaded to send rarely used toys to a donation center if they know another child needs them.

USE IT UP
WEAR IT OUT
MAKE DO OR
DO WITHOUT

CHAPTER 7

Clutter Is Normal—Be Weird

....

Are you ready to part with your clutter? Do you look forward to enjoying your home more starting now, and even more in the years to come? I really want that for you, too.

My own story is pretty typically American. I grew up spending my free time in malls. I made the weekly pilgrimage to the big box stores for necessities, and always brought home extra junk that seemed to jump in my cart. When I had kids, their stuff seemed to overtake the entire house, and then their stuff had stuff kittens, or at least dust bunnies. I bought a bigger car to hold and haul it. I went to consignment stores and got great deals on more children's clothing than we really needed. I was being frugal and economically responsible, but that was only half of the story.

I was surviving and keeping an organized house by making weekly or monthly trips to donation centers. I was filling my car with all the things that I had dragged into the house weeks earlier. My family does a pretty good job of keeping our landfill trash to a minimum, but our recycling load was even too much. At some point, the convenience of online shopping created the burden of too many boxes a week in our home, which had to be regularly broken down and hauled to the curb for recycling. It was exhausting.

And that's only the stuff that we actively purchased at the store. Then there's all the other stuff that the schools wanted us to buy, that we picked up as "free" gifts on our travels to community and cultural events, gifts from family, and crafts that my kids made. There were many more places that stuff kept coming from, even without buying it. You get the idea. It's easy to accept this flow of stuff through our lives and homes as normal.

When I started aggressively refusing unwanted stuff, I gained control of the stuff that we owned. Little things, like refusing bags at the checkout line. Who needs a bag to carry a pack of gum and a bottle of water from the convenience store? Heck, who needs the bottle of water? I carry a refillable water bottle everywhere. It's become as automatic to me as grabbing my purse on the way out the door. My kids know that if they don't grab their own water bottles, I won't be buying them a drink on the road.

I will gladly purchase consumable fundraisers, like Girl Scout Cookies. But I have been known to write a check as a donation instead of purchasing gift wrap or other items from schools and clubs. I don't purchase the pricey school spirit gear because my kids are sure to grow out of it in the next five minutes, and then it becomes clutter. (Yes, I realize that some people keep t-shirts as memorabilia. I've helped clients organize boxes and boxes of them. Do yourself a favor, and make them into a quilt that you can use and enjoy every day, and free up that storage space.)

Early on, my strategies around stuff were really focused on debt and finances. By reducing purchases, staying out of malls, and enforcing my own 24-hour rule, I bought less. I paid less. I owed less.

Later, my stuff reduction strategies took on more of an eco-friendly tone. I was saving trees, reducing my family's footprint, choosing items that weren't over-packaged. I was helping the planet by not accepting free items that would go right into the trash.

These days, it's more about the fact that I only have so much time and energy to devote to managing and cleaning stuff, and it just wears me out some days. My preference—and this doesn't have to be your preference—is to have fewer things, but things of higher quality. I'd rather have three really great sweaters than a dozen that I don't love.

How will you know when you've succeeded at your organizing efforts? There is no finish line. There is no one final day when you will say, "I'm done!" But each organizing project you complete at home, and each item that you choose NOT to buy or bring home can be a victory.

STOP CLUTTER IN ITS TRACKS

Don't just get better at decluttering

HeartWork
organizing

If there is one thing I want you to take away from this book, it is that you will finally feel organized not when you are chucking things out the door, but when you are happy with what is coming into your life. By getting control over your physical clutter, you'll have more time, you won't be swimming in overwhelming paper piles, and you'll be spending less money.

You can make all of these changes.

You can have a more organized home.

You can have a more peaceful life.

Use these questions to help you continue to develop your organizing muscle and get closer to your goals:

- Do I feel good about the amount of bags, boxes and deliveries that come into my home? Or is it an effort to carry, unbox and dispose of packaging?

- Do I feel happy when I completely wear through or get as much use from an item as possible?

- Are other people in my household able to put things in their assigned place most of the time?

- If I moved tomorrow, would I be willing to pay someone to pack, transport and unpack this?

- Am I able to entertain angels, or does clutter stop me from being hospitable and entertaining guests in my home?

You now have a solid five-step system to follow again and again and again.

Start with a written goal

Organize by group

Reduce, release, reset

Tweak and enhance

Succeed and Celebrate

Download a handy, free printable at http://SORT.heartworkorg.com.

SORT AND SUCCEED

- Start
- Organize into groups
- Reduce, Release, Reset
- Tweak and enhance
- Succeed and Celebrate

If you have a specific question or situation, search

http://HeartWorkOrg.com

to see if I've written about it already. You can also email me directly. Even better, we hope to see you and hear about your organizing projects in the Clutter-Free Facebook Group, where you can interact with me and lots of other people who are also using SORT and Succeed.

https://www.facebook.com/groups/heartworkorganizing/

Are you inspired to start your real-life organizing project right away, but still need personal guidance? Contact the HeartWork Organizing team for virtual organizing appointments, wherever you are in the world. Visit http://SORT.HeartWorkOrg.com.

I can't wait to hear what organizing project you are going to tackle first. I honestly want you to succeed.

You can SORT and Succeed!

Review

....

You've just succeeded by making it all the way to the end of this book. If it has helped you, please take just a quick moment to leave a review. This is absolutely the best way to help other people who want to get organized using the SORT and Succeed system.

It doesn't have to be long or perfect (we're done with perfectionism, after all). Thanks for adding your review.

Acknowledgments

....

My biggest literary achievement so far is not that I have published two books, but that my husband and I have raised two girls who love to read. Perhaps they will go on to write books of their own, and hopefully they will start much sooner than I did. I am extraordinarily grateful to the girls and my wonderful husband, since most of this book was written while recovering from foot surgery. That meant they put up with me being horizontal for weeks and busy completing this book all in the same year. While it doesn't sound ideal, it proves we can have a good time as long as we are together, just like the Berenstain Bears.

Many of my colleagues had a part in bringing this book to the world. Wendy Eden, Melinda Hollis, Mollie Bartelt and Cathi Nelson all said just the right things at the right time. The lovely Megan Wing was absolutely indispensable in the home stretch. My merry band of early readers were an enormous help, including Michelle Atchison, Allison Hallam, Maria Reyes, Jennifer Oxenford, Susan Tabor-Kleiman and Kathleen Thomas. Thanks to Dr. Mlodzienski for a new foot and six weeks on the couch to write this book. The wonderful Jim Haupt provided more technical support than anyone should need during their book launch. Gremlins tremble at his name.

But most of all, this book is about and for and in honor of the hundreds of people and families who have allowed me and my staffers to come into their homes. It is always a blessing to be able to help you, learn from you and become your friend. Thank you from the bottom of my bins and my heart. We are truly honored to bring our heartwork to your lives.